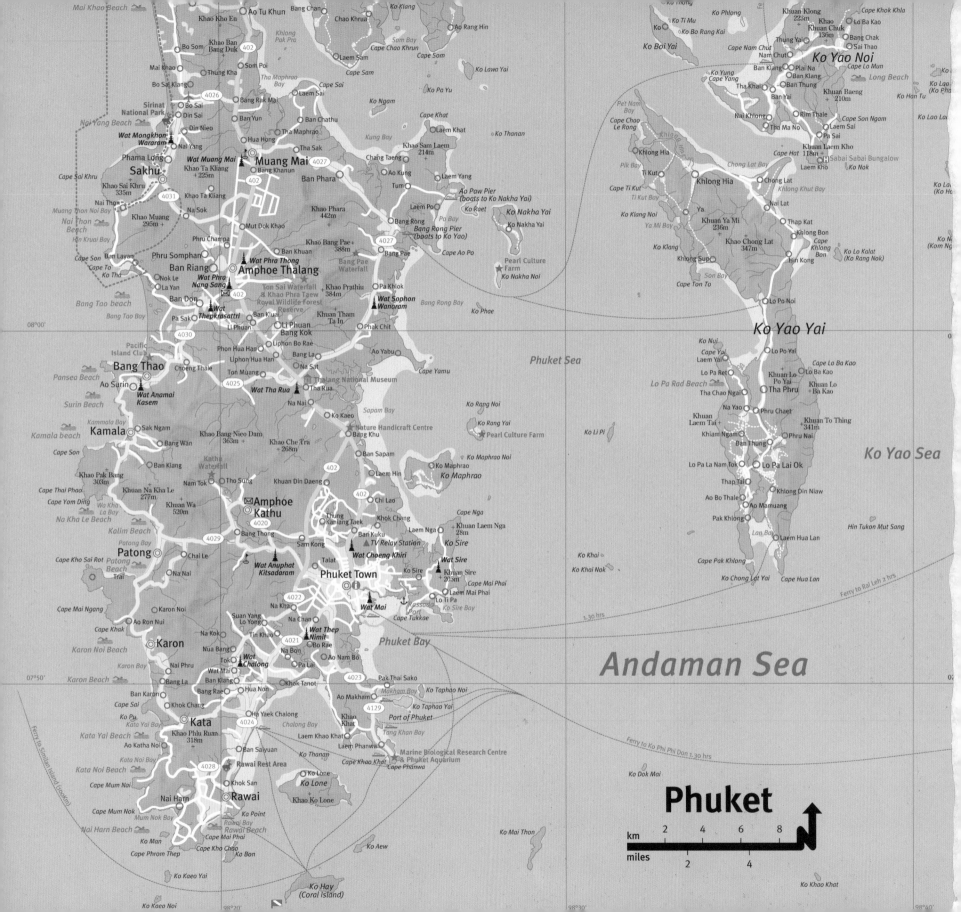

Phuket
PEARL OF THE ORIENT

Photographs by Bill Wassman & Alberto Cassio

Text by William Warren

PERIPLUS EDITIONS
Singapore • Hong Kong • Indonesia

Published by Periplus Editions (HK) Ltd

www.periplus.com

ISBN: 978-0-7946-0129-4

Distributed by
North America, Latin America and Europe
Tuttle Publishing
364 Innovation Drive, North Clarendon, VT 05759-9436, USA
Tel: 1 (802) 773-8930, Fax: 1 (802) 773-6993
info@tuttlepublishing.com
www.tuttlepublishing.com

Japan
Tuttle Publishing
Yaekari Building, 3rd Floor, 5-4-12 Osaki, Shinagawa-ku, Tokyo 141 0032
Tel: (81) 3 5437-0171, Fax: (81) 3 5437-0755
sales@tuttle.co.jp
www.tuttle.co.jp

Asia Pacific
Berkeley Books Pte Ltd
61 Tai Seng Avenue, #02-12, Singapore 534167
Tel: (65) 6280 1330, Fax: (65) 6280-6290
inquiries@periplus.com.sg
www.periplus.com.sg

15 14 13 12   10 9 8 7 6 5 4 3 2

Printed in Malaysia   1201TW

Front endpaper: Coconut palms fringe Phuket's western beaches, where sunsets can be spectacular.
Back endpaper: Shaded beach chairs provide comfort for bathers on a typical stretch of sand in Phuket.
Right: Dancer in a khon mask performing in a Thai classical dance drama.
Opposite: Fishing boats docked at one of the scenic beaches of Ko Phi Phi, a popular retreat near Phuket.

Contents

Discovering Paradise 4

Phuket's History 12

Phuket's Alluring Towns and Beaches 22

Side Trips Out of Phuket 36

Phuket's Inland Attractions 58

Visiting Phuket 70

"Phuket today offers a diversity of attractions, with something to appeal to almost any type of traveler. There are the famous beaches, of course, with their varying moods and accommodations, ranging from modest to the last word in luxury."

Discovering Paradise

Back in the early 1970s, the American magazine *Newsweek* ran a special feature on destinations for travelers in search of something new, untouched and unspoiled. The only entry suggested for Thailand was the island of Phuket, then known primarily to an adventurous handful of backpackers willing to endure assorted hardships for the pleasures of pristine white-sand beaches where they were unlikely to encounter any of the usual visitors who insisted on such amenities as proper hotels with bathrooms, room service, and running water.

Thais, of course, had long been aware of this large island in the Andaman Sea off the southern peninsula that extends all the way to Malaysia. Thanks to its tin mines and coconut plantations, as well as its more exotic products like pearls and edible birds' nests, it long enjoyed a reputation as the second richest province in the country after Bangkok (it is now ranked third) and was thus a major

contributor to the national treasury. Comparatively few, however, had ever actually been there, and even fewer had ever given much thought to its potential for mass tourism.

There were several reasons for this neglect. Phuket is located some 931 kilometers from Bangkok. At that point, the railway to the Malaysian border runs along the opposite side of the peninsula, making direct contact difficult, and until the Sarasin Bridge was built at the upper tip of the island in the late 1960s, the only way of getting there was by ferry boat. The sole settlement of any size was Phuket Town on the lower southeastern side of the island, which had some handsome old Sino-European mansions but only a few rather basic hotels for the casual visitor.

The rest of the island, which covers some 52 square kilometers—it is considerably larger than either Penang or Manhattan—consisted of steep granite hills and dense vegetation, either primary jungle or immense rubber and coconut plantations. (The name Phuket comes from the Malay word for "hill," *bukit*.) A few unpaved roads led to open tin mines but otherwise travel across to the west coast by car was difficult and almost impossible in the rainy season. Although there was an airport, built by the Japanese during the Second World War, it was still fairly primitive and plane services were erratic.

Page 5: Peaceful beach on Ko Racha, an island just off the coast of Phuket.
Left, top: Rubber, once the chief crop of Phuket, is grown in large plantations.
Left, bottom: Latex, once extracted from the trees, is pressed into sheets and hung out to dry in the sun.
Right: Dramatic limestone cliffs offer a challenge to rock climbers in the neighboring province of Krabi.

All this changed with dramatic speed as word spread of the charms of the 12 major beaches and numerous smaller coves of the western coast, which just happened to coincide with a drop in tin and rubber prices and thus the need to find a new source of revenue. Beginning with Mai Khao, over which planes fly on their way in to the airport, and continuing around the island's southern tip to Rawai, each of these has a distinctive atmosphere to complement their crystal clear waters, pearly white beaches, and verdant foliage. Some are perfectly shaped crescents, protected at either end by huge, dramatic boulders, while others are immensely long stretches of sand. When the *Newsweek* article appeared, the only beach that had been developed to any great extent was Patong, which was also the nearest to the capital city.

Local entrepreneurs were the first to respond to the increase in visitors, prompted not only by the enthusiasm of backpackers but also by a growing network of better roads in southern Thailand and more regular air service from Bangkok. They built simple bungalows for rent during the dry season and a few hotels, the most modern of which, oddly, had scenic views from its hilltop site but no direct access to a beach. (Guests were bussed down and back to one for the day.)

The first well-known chain to come to Phuket was the Club Méditerranée, which opened a sprawling, low-rise complex on Kata Yai Beach in 1986. M. L. Tri Devakul, one

Left: A yacht at anchor in the bay of Phra Nang Beach at Krabi.
Right, top: Terrace of the Phuket Yacht Club, overlooking Nai Harn Beach.
Right, bottom: A scrumptious buffet spread at the Club Méditerranée, the first resort to be opened on Kata Beach.

Left: Water scootering and parasailing are two popular sports at Patong, the first of Phuket's beaches to be opened to tourists.

Opposite, top: Beachfront at Patong, noted for its shopping and lively nightlife.

Opposite, bottom: Kata Beach, with a small, private-owned offshore island.

of Thailand's leading architects and a pioneer in the island's upscale development, who designed the central buildings of this resort, also built the luxurious Phuket Yacht Club on Nai Harn Beach, followed by Le Meridien on a small, self-contained inlet popularly known as Relax Bay between Patong and Karon. In the next decade and a half, other major hotels appeared on almost all the west coast beaches, and modern roads replaced the old dirt trails that once provided the only link between them. There are currently even signs of interest in the less popular beaches along the east coast. Phuket also acquired an international airport which now receives regular flights not only from Bangkok but also from Singapore and distant Europe.

Phuket today offers a diversity of attractions, with something to appeal to almost any type of traveler. There are the famous beaches, of course, with their varying moods and accommodations, ranging from modest to the last word in luxury. There are also family-style amusement parks, world-class golf courses, health spas, facilities for marine sports of all kinds, restaurants serving the full range of Thai cuisine, shops selling treasures from most parts of the country, and opportunities for excursions to nearby attractions.

Though some of the development, especially in the early years, has been haphazard and inspired simply by greed, the government has come to realize that much of Phuket's appeal to international travelers lies in its natural beauty. It tends to listen to the assorted groups of environmentalists who campaign for better conservation of its natural assets and to resort operators who argue for the need for quality over quantity.

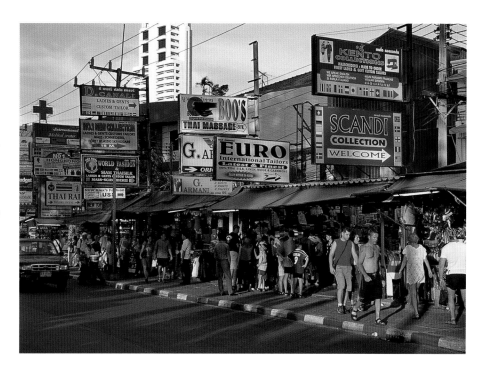

Phuket's History

"Phuket, or Junkceylon, was strategically located on an important trading route between India and China and this, in addition to its varied natural resources, soon made it well known to outsiders."

First Edition 1893
Second Edition 1976

design by Chuang Mulpinit

G. E. GERINI
BANGKOK
1893

CHULĂKANTAMANGALA
or
The Tonsure Ceremony
As Performed in Siam

THE SIAM SOCIETY
UNDER ROYAL PATRONAGE
1976

"The early history of the island is wrapped in deep mystery," wrote Colonel G. E. Gerini in a pioneering 1905 monograph on Phuket published in the *Siam Society Journal*, and to a large extent that still applies today. Some evidence of neolithic habitation has been found at Takua Pa, north of the island, as well as at nearby Phang Nga and Krabi. It is also believed that the earliest historical inhabitants were a primitive, seminomadic people called Chao Nam, "water people," by modern Thais or Chao Le, "sea people," because of their notable skills at swimming and deep-sea diving.

There is some confusion, too, about the name Junkceylon (in a variety of spellings) by which the island was known until relatively modern times. ("Phuket," adapted from the Malay word *bukit*, meaning "hill" or "height," only came into use in the late 18th century, shortly before Bangkok was established as the Thai capital.) *Hobson-Jobson*, an entertaining survey of Anglo-Indian words and phrases by

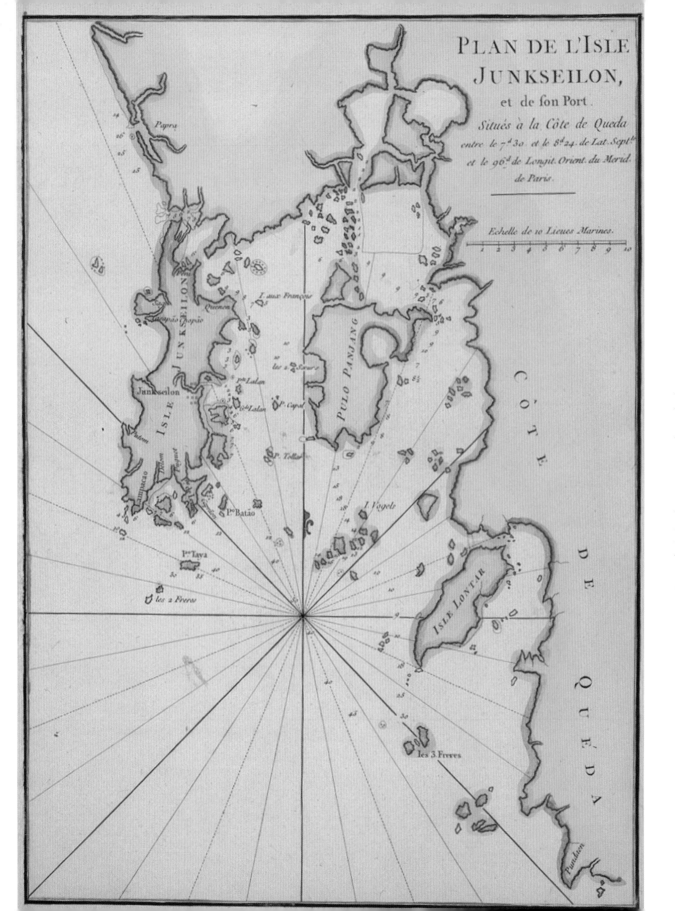

PLAN DE L'ISLE
JUNKSEILON,
et de fon Port.

Situés à la Côte de Queda
entre le 7.d 30. et le 8.d 24. de Lat. Sept.le
et le 96.d de Longit. Orient. du Merid.
de Paris.

Echelle de 10 Lieues Marines.

Page 12: Man wearing a southern-style sarong, common dress for Phuket people in the old days.
Page 13: Earliest account of Phuket in English, published by the Siam Society. The man pictured on the left-hand page is Colonel G. E. Gernini, who wrote the monograph.
Left: Old French map of Phuket, using one of the several spellings of its former name. Probably dating from the late 17th century, when the French briefly played an active role in the island's history.
Opposite: Chinese junk of the type that once came to Phuket in large numbers for trade when the monsoon winds were favorable.

Henry Yule and A. C. Burnell, published in 1886, offers two possible derivations. One is that it comes from Ujong Salang (*ujong* being a Malay word for "headland" and *salang* possibly a variant of Thalang, the island's principal settlement), while the other claims that *jong* means "junk," a Chinese sailing vessel, and *salang*, when applied to boats, means "heavily tossing."

Whatever the answer to these conundrums, Phuket, or Junkceylon, was strategically located on an important trading route between India and China, and this, in addition to its varied natural resources, soon made it well known to outsiders. Tin ore, as prized in the ancient world as it is today, was so abundant that it could be easily extracted from veins near the surface, and before the mines of Malaysia were opened Phuket was the major source of supply in the region. There were other treasures as well, such as ambergris, ivory, rhinoceros horn, and rare corals, either on the island or the nearby mainland. Most desirable of all, at least to Chinese traders as early as the Sung Dynasty, were the edible birds' nests deposited by tiny swifts in lofty caves, much esteemed for their alleged medicinal and aphrodisiac powers.

The Chao Nam, sometimes known as Sea Gypsies, are believed by some anthropologists to have come originally from Indonesia. A number of small groups still live on the island, with their own language and culture, though they are increasingly being assimilated into the majority population and may disappear entirely before too long.

Thai influence began to be felt in the far south in the late 13th century, during the reign of King Ramkhamhaeng of Sukhothai, the first independent Thai capital. Actual power,

however, remained tenuous for a long time, partly because of the distance and partly because of fierce pirates who used the island as a base while marauding in the Bay of Bengal. During the Ayutthaya period, increased control was exerted: the export of tin became a royal monopoly, and Phuket was assigned to the same *monthon* or administrative area as Nakhon Sri Thammarat on the other side of the peninsula, which had a long history as a cultural center.

Europeans turned up on the scene soon after the sea route to India was discovered by Vasco da Gama in the early 16th century. For a short time, beginning in 1626, the Dutch East India Company was granted mining concessions on the island by King Song Tham of Ayutthaya, but this came to an end when local people complained of mistreatment and rose up against the Dutch.

They were followed by the French toward the end of the same century. Simon de la Loubère, who led an embassy

from the court of Louis XIV to Ayutthaya in 1687, mentions the tin mines of Phuket in an account he wrote of his trip and notes that a French medical missionary named Brother René Charbonneau served as governor of the island from 1681 to 1685, an appointment probably devised by the Thais as a way of discouraging other European powers in the area, especially the British and the Dutch, who might be tempted to move in.

Still more Frenchmen appeared in 1689 following a violent revolution that led to the expulsion of most foreigners from the capital. French forces from Pondicherry threatened to retaliate by occupying the island, and General Desfarges, who had been in command of troops in Ayutthaya, arrived with 332 men, demanding enough tin to compensate for his losses. The Thais refused to cooperate and Desfarges wisely decided to withdraw; he perished in a storm on his homeward voyage.

For most of the next century, Phuket remained in a state of semianarchy, theoretically under Thai control but in reality beset by pirates who discouraged systematic trading. Captain Alexander Hamilton, a Scottish adventurer who came to the region early in the 18th century, made the following observations:

"Between Mergee [Mergui] and Jonkceyloan [sic] there are several good harbours for shipping, but the sea coast is very thin of inhabitants, because there are great numbers of

Girl in southern-style costume against a seaside background, probably early 19th century.

Freebooters, called Salleiters, who inhabit islands along the sea coast and they both rob and take people for slaves and transport them for Atchen and there make sale of them and Jonkceyloan often feels the weight of their depredations.

"The north end of Jonkceyloan lies within a mile of the continent... Between the island and the continent is a good harbour for shipping in the southwest monsoons, and on the west side of the island Puton [Patong] bay is a safe harbour in the northeast winds. The islands afford good masts for shipping, and abundance of tin, but few people to dig for it, by reason of the aforementioned outlaws and the governors, being mostly Chinese, who buy their places at the court of Siam and, to reimburse themselves, oppress the people."

Despite such reports, the island seems to have enjoyed a moderate degree of prosperity and to have attracted Europeans as well as Thais and Malays. Its capital was Thalang, in the northern half, now merely a few shophouses on the road leading from the airport, while the second largest settlement was Tha Rua, a little further south. (*Tha* is the Thai word for "port" or "landing stage.")

Ayutthaya fell to the Burmese in 1767 and was almost completely destroyed, but under the leadership of King Taksin the Thais rallied, expelled the enemy, and established a temporary capital at Thonburi, across the Chao Phraya River from a prosperous little trading center called Bangkok. In 1782, King Rama I assumed the throne and founded the present Chakri Dynasty. One of his first decisions was to move the capital to Bangkok, where he hoped to recreate the splendors of the lost Ayutthaya.

While these momentous events were taking place far away, an adventurous Englishman named Francis Light first appeared off the southern coast. Though a freelance merchant whose principal aim was making money, he also had connections with the British East India Company, which at the time was looking for suitable trading ports in the region. One of the places he looked at was the island of Penang, which then belonged to the Malay state of Kedah. Negotiations with the Sultan proved difficult, however, and in 1771 Light turned his attentions to Phuket.

Phuket held other attractions for him besides trade. On an early visit to Kedah, he had met a girl named Martinha Rosells, a beauty of Siamese/Portuguese extraction who came from a Portuguese community that originally lived in Phuket but was later forced to move to Kedah. She and Light never officially married but they had five children and remained together until his death. She also went with him when he returned to Phuket and they set up house in Tha Rua, which was then a bustling little town close to the sea. According to one account, it had "a large Portuguese settlement, as well as a fine market street, composed of large brick buildings, among which rose the spacious houses belonging to the Europeans that used to reside here while their ships lay at anchor in the harbor."

The Lights' house, of which no trace remains today, has been described as being "built of brick, plastered with lime mixed with a reddish dye from the laterite soil so common on the island. This gave it a slightly pinkish color which was cheerful without being glaring. The main walls were

[ฝระยาพิไล่ยสุ่จทุรการ]   [ฝระยาส่ถาวรถลางกูล]

ศึกถลาง เมื่อ พ.ศ. 2328 กองทัพพม่าได้ยกมาล้อมเมืองถลางไว้ คุณหญิงจันภรรยาเจ้าเมืองและคุณแพ่งมุกน้องสาวได้นำน้ำถ่าวถลางออกต่อสู้พม่า จนพม่า
ผ่ายแพ้กลับไป. PRINCESS SRISUNTORN IN B.E. 2328 (A.D.1775) THE BURMESE ARMY BESIEG THE TOWN OF THALANG THE LADY YINGCHUN THE
WIFE OF THE GOVERNOR AND LADY MOOK HER YOUNGER SISTER LEAD THE PEOPLE OF THALANG AGAINS THE BURMESE TILL THEY WERE BEATEN -RETURNED TO BURMA.

about 12 feet high with a steeply pitched thatched roof…. [It] had few windows or doors, which in any case opened onto the veranda and were closed with wooden shutters at night against predators, either animal or human…. During the day the main door, a stout double leaf wooden one, was always open allowing light and air into the house. An open back door also added to the ventilation. The house was however still gloomy which added to its coolness and comfort, though it was little used by day except for a large English style breakfast in the morning and a heavy dinner at about 3 pm in the afternoon."

Here, Martinha gave birth to their first child, Sarah, in 1779, and here, too, they lived an active social life, becoming

Above: Phuket's two heroines fighting against the Burmese, during an invasion in the late 18th century. Detail from a mural in a temple near Thalang.

friends of the Governor of Thalang and his wife Lady Chan. She was often alone, though, for Francis was usually away on regular trading voyages. He continued to vacillate between advocating the acquisition of either Phuket or Penang as a British port—at times he pressed for both—but finally decided in favor of Penang, where he founded a permanent settlement in July 1786 and thus passed out of Phuket's history. (One legend, probably apocryphal, claims that Martinha influenced his decision in order to save her homeland from European domination.)

A year earlier, however, he may have provided some crucial assistance to his friend Lady Chan. Burma, Thailand's old enemy, was again threatening the kingdom and enjoyed a series of victories in the south. Toward the end of 1785, they laid siege to Thalang, where the situation became desperate due to the sudden death of the Governor. Lady Chan wrote to Light asking for his help, and he is said to have responded by sending supplies of both ammunition and food.

In any event, she and her equally redoubtable sister, Mook, took charge of the town's defenses. Sir Arthur Payne, an English historian, comments as follows: "They assembled men and built two large stockades wherewith to protect the town. The dowager governess and her maiden sister displayed great bravery and fearlessly faced the enemy. They urged the officials and the people, both males and females, to fire the ordnance and muskets and led them day after day in sorties out of the stockades to fight the Burmese. So the latter were unable to reduce the town and after a month's vain attempts, provisions failing them, they had to withdraw."

In appreciation of their bravery, King Rama I conferred a noble title on Lady Chan, making her Lady Tepsiri, while Mook became Tao Srisuntorn. The two heroines are commemorated with larger-than-life bronze statues that stand today on the airport road, not far from where their battles took place, and an annual fair is held in their honor each March.

The Burmese returned in 1809, and this time, after a siege that lasted 27 days, they reduced Thalang to ruins. When they were again driven out, a new town called Phuket developed further south. Eventually, this became the provincial capital and the center of its wealth as the threat of further invasions receded and the British finally brought piracy under control.

A literary view of Phuket in the early 19th century is found in an account by Nai Mi, the favorite pupil of Thailand's greatest poet, Sunthorn Phu. Nai Mi was a Buddhist monk at Bangkok's Wat Po at the time he took his arduous journey, probably around 1840. He exercises considerable poetic license in his description of the seashore ("Water snakes and mermaids dart forth, in a swinging zig-zag gait, to disport themselves with their mates or swim past by close pairs in unbroken procession"), but is fairly realistic in describing the town and its people. "The islanders … love to dress tidily and tastefully," he says. "Handsomely built damsels are in evidence; but, awe-struck, I dare not glance upon them. For I am deeply afraid of their subtle philters and craftily concocted charms that so easily lead to perdition." (In his monograph, Col. Gerini helpfully explains this observation: "Women from the southern provinces of Siam on the Malay peninsula are reputed to be exceedingly skillful in the preparation of love

philters and charms; hence their occult craft is much feared by people from the capital and other northern districts.")

Throughout the rest of the century and into the 20th, as Thailand liberalized its trade restrictions through a series of treaties with Western powers, Phuket's growth was extraordinary. With the encouragement of a visionary governor, Phraya Ratsadamupradit Mahitsarapakdi, who was in command from 1901 to 1913, Chinese immigrants arrived in ever-increasing numbers to work the tin mines, some from nearby Penang and others all the way from China itself; one estimate claims that around 30,000 were thus employed by the end of the reign of King Rama V (1868–1910). Diligent and hardworking, some of them acquired large fortunes and

Above: Impressive bronze statues of Lady Chan and her sister Mook at a memorial located on the road leading in from the airport.

built imposing mansions in a blend of Western and Chinese architecture, usually called Sino-Portuguese since it first appeared in such early colonies as Malacca and Macao.

Another result of the Chinese immigration that continues to play a prominent role in Phuket is the annual Vegetarian Festival. This seems to have begun around 1825 at a settlement called Baan Katun in the centrally located Khatu district. Thickly forested in those days, the area was notorious for its deadly fevers, which felled large numbers of tin miners as

Above: Sino-Portuguese shophouse in the town of Phuket, with Chinese-style doors and windows, dating from the 19th century.

well as occasional visitors. Among the latter was a touring Chinese opera company that stayed almost a year, putting on nightly shows for the miners. When they also came down with fever, some of the cast recalled an ancient Chinese custom of turning vegetarian for a period of time, usually during the ninth month of the lunar calendar, and suggested that this might improve their fortunes.

Accordingly, a rather simplified version of the ceremony was staged and proved so successful that it became an annual event, not only at Kathu Temple but at all the other important Chinese temples on the island, held in October. Certain elements have been borrowed from Hindu ritual and incorporated into the nine-day festival, the most notable among them being self-inflicted ordeals such as walking over red-hot coals or up razor-sharp ladders and piercing the flesh with sharp rods.

Some 60 percent of Phuket's population today is either Thai or Thai-Chinese. Nevertheless, as in the rest of southern Thailand, Islam is a powerful influence and as many mosques as Buddhist and Chinese temples can be seen on the island. As noted above, there are still small communities of Chao Nam, who continue to demonstrate their skills at diving, fishing, and scaling slender bamboo ladders to collect birds' nests, as esteemed as ever by Chinese gourmets.

The first rubber trees, introduced from Malaya, were planted in 1903 and within a short time had not only provided an important new industry but had also transformed the island's landscape as once-dense native forests gave way to large plantations. Other crops, such as cashew nuts, coconuts, and pineapples, also proved profitable. By 1933, when it became a separate province, Phuket was the most prosperous in Thailand outside of Bangkok.

In spite of such progress, however, which included one of the best-equipped hospitals in the country, it remained culturally closer to Penang and Malaya than to the distant capital. Rich Chinese families in Phuket tended to send their children to Penang for education, much of the trade was with foreigners, and though King Rama V himself visited the island toward the end of his reign, not many of his ordinary subjects made the long journey. Thus, when Colonel Gerini wrote his historical study for the Siam Society early in the last century, and when an American missionary named John Carrington offered a contemporary report to the Society a year later, they were describing a place almost unknown.

This did not really change until the late 1960s when the construction of all-weather highways and a bridge linking the island with the mainland made Phuket much more easily accessible; an airport originally built by the Japanese during the Second World War brought still more outsiders. All this coincided with a decline in tin production from open mines, most of which had been exhausted, and increasing use of more sophisticated offshore facilities. By the 1970s, Phuket was ready to apply its long-established business acumen to developing a new source of wealth through mass tourism.

Right, top: Woman standing at the gate of one of the old houses in Phuket Town, built in a mixture of Western and Chinese styles.
Right, bottom: Detail of a modern building in the town that seeks to evoke the style common to older architecture.

"What draws most modern-day visitors to Phuket is not its city sites or its agriculture but its fabled beaches. All the best ones lie on the western side of the island on the Andaman Sea, starting in the north and curving around the southern tip."

Phuket's Alluring Towns and Beaches

Phuket today, in a number of highly visible ways, is a very different place from the bucolic island those early backpackers "discovered" in their search for empty beaches and quiet serenity. It has more people, for one thing, not only a substantial number of the eight million tourists who come to Thailand every year but also numerous Thais who have migrated from every part of the country to participate in the latest boom. Along major roads there is less natural scenery as, increasingly, rice fields, rubber plantations, and even abandoned tin mines make way for new buildings—housing estates, row shops, entertainment facilities, and the latest development, vast superstores—which seem to spring almost overnight in many of the more popular areas. On the beaches, more than 500 hotels have been built, most of them in the last decade. All this might prompt some old-timers to conclude that yet another Eden has been lost to the forces of mass tourism and an eagerness to cash in on it in any way possible.

Yet, appearances can be misleading. Phuket has inevitably changed as it has developed into Thailand's most popular travel destination. At the same time, however, much of its legendary charm remains intact if one takes the time to look for it, and not all the changes have been necessarily for the worse.

The first obvious improvement is the new airport, completed only a few years ago but already scheduled for further expansion. Sleek, modern, and efficient, it is now one of four outside Bangkok with facilities for international travel and serves numerous flights every day. Also greatly superior to its hazardous predecessor is the expanded highway that leads to the provincial capital through the old center of Thalang and past the imposing monument marking the spot where the island's two heroines made their courageous stand in 1786.

Phuket Town currently has a population of around 50,000, which is rapidly increasing. There is talk of upgrading its status from that of *tessabaan muang* (town) to *tessabaan nakhon* (city), which would provide the town with increased autonomy and greater ability to cope with the inevitable problems arising from rapid development. Nowadays, Phuket Town consists mostly of new buildings, some of considerable height, but the majority in the form of the low, rather dowdy, standardized row shops common to all Thai towns and cities.

Here and there, though, there are still architectural treasures to be discovered. Some of the shophouses date from the early 19th century and display elaborately carved doors and windows in

Shop on a street in Phuket Town, built in a mixture of Chinese and Western styles. Thousands of Chinese came to the island in the 19th century to work in the tin mines.

the Chinese style. Similarly, a number of the grand old Sino-Portuguese mansions (referred to by older residents as *angmor-lao*, *angmor* being a Chinese word for "foreign" and *lao* for "large house") can still be seen, usually set in spacious gardens and displaying elegant arches, stucco decorations, and Victorian fretwork. Too often these are apt to be in a somewhat dilapidated state, the cost of maintaining them being beyond the current owners' means, but a few have been restored and registered as landmarks by the Fine Arts Department.

One of the town's oldest and most handsome structures is the stately Government House, built during the reign of King Rama V, which has numerous tall doors (99 by one count) and only two windows. The colonial elegance of the building inspired the producers of *The Killing Fields* to request permission to use it in the award-winning film, where it plays a prominent role as the French Embassy in Phnom Penh. Just across the street stands another impressive building in the same style, dating from 1916, which serves as the Provincial Court.

The busiest public market in town is along Rasada Street, especially active in the early morning when local residents prefer to do their shopping. Stalls offer a wide assortment of fruit and vegetables (mangoes, mangosteens, rambutans, finger-sized bananas, papayas, coconuts, pineapples of exceptional sweetness, cashew nuts, and a pungent bean called *satao*, which Phuket people love (but which is very much of an acquired taste for most visitors); spices and culinary herbs used in southern cooking (chili peppers, of course, along with

Right, top: Old Western colonial-style building dating from the 19th century.
Right, bottom: Public market in Phuket Town, where local products and foodstuffs are on sale daily.

lemongrass, sweet basil, tamarind, garlic and ginger); fresh meat and fish; household goods of all kinds; and fragrant, intricately woven garlands used as offerings at local shrines and temples.

The freshest seafood is available at the port of Phuket, a short drive east of the town, where commercial fishing boats unload their nightly catch of fish, squid, lobster, shrimp, crab, and other items early each morning. Some of it ends up in restaurants all over the island, but most goes by refrigerated containers straight to Bangkok and other parts of the country.

A pleasant place to escape the bustle of the provincial capital, popular with many residents for lunch and in the late afternoon, is Khao Rang, the tallest of several hills in the town. The upper levels have been turned into a Fitness Park, with exercise equipment and attractive landscaped gardens, and near the top are several restaurants offering panoramic views of the port and the sea.

On the way to and from the town, in almost any direction, one passes through rubber plantations, both vast and small, their trees stretching in long, regimented rows that cast a perpetual, somewhat eerie shade. Since the first *Hevea brasiliensis* trees were brought from Malaysia in 1903, new hybrids have been introduced that grow faster and yield more latex, but the procedure of tapping is still basically the same as that pioneered by Henry Nicholas Ridley, a director of the Singapore Botanic Gardens, toward the end of the 19th century. A slashed incision is made in the trunk in the early morning, and the thick white sap drips slowly into a cup attached below. The full cups are collected in the afternoon and poured into large trays where they harden into sheets of latex. Further processing is done either on the rubber estate or at several large facilities operated by private companies. There is also a government rubber experimental station on the airport road, which works on developing new and improved techniques.

Other crops commonly seen around the island are the ubiquitous coconut palm, almost every part of which serves some useful purpose, from food to building materials; pineapples, often grown in between rows of young rubber trees while they are maturing and famous for their natural sweetness; cashew trees bearing large fruits, each of which has a single curved nut dangling from the bottom; and fast-growing oil palms, the most recent introduction, with dark-green spreading fronds.

Food vendors sell a variety of fresh and cooked local dishes, many of them incorporating local seafood.

Here and there, old abandoned tin mines reveal themselves in the form of expanses of raw red soil, sometimes enhanced by deep green lakes but strangely barren of the luxuriant vegetation otherwise so prevalent, even many years after the last bits of valuable ore have been extracted from them.

What draws most modern visitors to Phuket, however, is not its city sights or its agriculture but its fabled beaches. All the best ones lie on the western side of the island on the Andaman Sea, starting in the north and curving around the southern tip. (East coast beaches, though they might appear tempting on a map, are often fringed by dense mangrove swamps or polluted by offshore tin dredging. Some, however, have possibilities and are currently being considered by resort developers, especially those incorporating marinas where private yachts can be docked. One of the most impressive is the Royal Phuket Marina, opened at the end of 2008, which not only has yacht facilities but also a hotel, condominium units, shops, a conference center, and a variety of high-end restaurants.) Until fairly recently, getting to the more desirable western side of the island took both time and effort, thanks to the lack of all-weather roads to much of it, but today a winding new highway leads along the coast and makes the journey far easier and more picturesque, if not necessarily shorter.

The first beaches one sees flying in to Phuket are the northernmost Mai Khao and Nai Yang, which together form a 16-kilometer stretch lined with tall, feathery casuarinas, among the relatively few trees able to withstand the strong, salty winds of the monsoon season. Alluring as they look from the air, however, these beaches are less satisfactory at ground level. At low tide, the water lacks the remarkable clarity found on the more southerly

beaches. Of greater concern to swimmers, the shore drops off steeply and unpredictable water currents can be dangerous during the monsoons. Nevertheless, a few major resorts have taken advantage of the natural beauty of the area and its closer proximity to the airport. Among the latest is the five-star J. W. Marriott, which sprawls over several landscaped acres, and not far away is the Blue Canyon Country Club, with one of the best of Phuket's several fine golf courses.

Above: Children's swimming pool, with fanciful features like turtles, at the J. W. Marriott resort on Nai Yang Beach.

A little further down at Bang Tao Beach, about eight kilometers long, something of an ecological miracle has taken place. This was once an exhausted tin mine, its soil so drained of nourishment it was long regarded as being unsuited to anything more than a cluster of budget tourist bungalows and a small Muslim fishing village at one end. Modern techniques, however, abetted by countless truckloads of new earth, have now transformed this stretch into a lush oasis of green, boasting the island's first fully integrated resort and one of the first of its kind anywhere in Southeast Asia.

Known as Phuket Laguna, the resort consists of five separate top-ranking hotels linked by waterways and tree-lined avenues and a spectacular golf course on the sea that has hosted a number of championship matches. The hotels include the Dusit Laguna, a low-rise facility with 226 rooms and suites; the internationally famous Banyan Tree, a luxurious Thai-style health spa cited by many surveys as being among the world's best; the Laguna Beach Resort; the Sheraton Grande Laguna; and the Allamanda Laguna, which offers longer-term serviced apartments. Guests at all of these can dine at any of the resort's 30 restaurants, shop at the Canal Village, and have free use of the boats and shuttle buses connecting them.

At the end of Bang Tao, a rocky finger of land juts out into the Andaman Sea and overlooks Surin Beach. This is the site of the Amanpuri, one of Phuket's most celebrated resorts and part of the Aman chain, which has facilities in many of the world's

Left: Chalong Bay, which provides a safe harbor for fishing boats.
Right, top: Golf course at the Banyan Tree, a luxurious Thai-style health spa.
Right, bottom: Swimming pool and beachfront at the Banyan Tree resort and spa.

other beauty spots. Airy Thai-style villas, most with their own pools and dining pavilions, offer the ultimate in pricey privacy for a jet-set clientele consisting of rock stars, fashion designers, and the merely rich. A more recent addition not far away, Trisara, offers similar charms, though the separate residences tend to be larger and more lavish.

Kamala, the next beach in the string, is a crescent of white sand bordered with jungle and coconut palms. In addition to several small resorts, it is also increasingly being used for some of the residential developments now offering serviced holiday homes for visitors who come to Phuket for more prolonged winter stays and prefer a place of their own. These are appearing all along the western coast and are proving popular with sun lovers from both nearby Singapore and more remote cities in Europe and America. Phuket FantaSea, a Disneyland-type attraction described elsewhere, is also located on Kamala.

Patong, some four kilometers long, was the first of Phuket's beaches to attract large numbers of tourists in the late 1980s and is still by far the most developed. It has dozens of hotels, large and small, as well as bungalow complexes to suit almost every budget, a gaudy maze of bars, discos, restaurants, and shops, and the island's only skyscraper, towering somewhat incongruously in the middle of it all. Though it may not appeal to anyone in search of a restful, quiet holiday, Patong is undeniably alluring to those who want a lively atmosphere and thus serves as the island's undisputed nightlife center. It is also the island's main centre for cheap shopping. The beach, despite it all, remains remarkably clean and is especially popular for a wide range of water sports like windsurfing, waterskiing, and parasailing.

Opposite: Aerial view of Phuket Laguna, an integrated resort created on the site of an old tin mine near Ban Tao Beach. **Right:** Pavilion at the Amanpuri, one of Phuket's most famous luxury resorts, consisting of a series of private Thai-style villas.

Left: Karon Beach, enclosed by a forested headland, boasts crystal-clear water.
Opposite, top: Le Meridien Hotel on Karon Noi Beach, sometimes called Relax Bay, designed by famous Phuket architect M. L. Tri Devakul.
Opposite, bottom: Kata Yai Beach. New buildings can be glimpsed going up on the far headland, while visiting yachts lie at anchor in the bay.

Steep hills and headlands (*laem* in Thai) formed by massive boulders separate these and other beaches down the coast so that each has been able to preserve its own special atmosphere, often strikingly different from one just a few kilometers away. Between glitzy Patong and the numerous facilities on long, straight Karon, for instance, is a small, secret cove known by some as Relax Bay (by others as Karon Noi), which has just one major hotel, Le Meredien Phuket, and its own virtually private sandy crescent. (No beach can be totally private, however, as affirmed by a series of angry protests during the early days of Phuket's development. Thus, a narrow pathway provides public access to Relax Bay, as well as to others in similarly isolated locations.)

Just beyond Karon lies Kata, divided into Kata Yai (Big Kata) and Kata Noi (Little Kata). In 1986, the Club Méditerranée opened on the former, becoming the first international group to select Phuket as a site. Following its usual policy of blending into the landscape as unobtrusively as possible, its low-rise buildings are almost hidden behind a dense screen of casuarina, pandanus, and other mostly indigenous trees and plants. At the other end of the same beach, also screened by trees, can be glimpsed the peaked roofs of Mom Tri's Boathouse, a boutique hotel with just 38 rooms and suites as well as a celebrated restaurant, an award-winning wine cellar, and weekly classes in Thai cooking. In early December, on the King's birthday, the Boathouse is the focus of the Phuket Regatta, an annual event that draws sailing enthusiasts from all over the region.

A single hotel, the Kata Thani, overlooks Kata Noi, along with a few bungalows scattered at the far end. Also overlooking the beach but from the top of the hill that separates the two Katas is

the stunning Mom Tri's Villa Royale, a relatively recent boutique facility that offers exceptional beauty and privacy. The property was formerly the private residence of architect M. L. Tri Devakul, a pioneer in Phuket resort development, and has been converted into an all-suites hotel, with rooms at various levels down the hillside and a saltwater swimming pool by the sea that incorporates natural boulders in its design, all surrounded by a luxuriant tropical garden. A fine, world-class restaurant, open to the public, attracts many outsiders as well as guests.

The last of Phuket's west coast beaches is Nai Harn, an idyllic stretch overlooked at its northern end by Le Royal Meredien Phuket Yacht Club, a deluxe hotel that climbs a steep hill to ensure a view from all its rooms. From here it is a short drive to Laen Phrom Thep, at the southernmost tip of the island. This grassy promontory is a favorite with both visitors and locals as a place to relax while watching the often spectacular sunsets and several picturesque offshore islands.

Around the cape lies quiet, palm-fringed Rawai Beach, the very first tourist beach on Phuket but today more a 'working beach,' on a rather shallow bay often filled with smaller fishing boats. Some of the last Chao Nam live peacefully in a village here, still regularly going out to demonstrate their skills at swimming and diving and still, twice a year (just after and just before the monsoon season), observing a festival called Loy Rua, during which miniature fishing boats are constructed and taken out to sea bearing offerings to the water spirits. Rawai is also a point of

Kata Thani Hotel on Kata Noi Beach. In the background can be seen some of the yachts gathered for the annual Phuket Regatta.

departure for boats going to several small offshore islands good for fishing and scuba diving, among them Ko Hae (known as Coral Island), Ko Lon, and Ko Mai Thon.

It was this coast that was hit by the notorious tsunami on the morning of December 26, 2004, following a major earthquake off the coast of Indonesia. Athough considerable damage was sustained at places like Kata, Patong, and Kamala, Phuket was spared the worst destruction of the massive waves because of its hilly topography. Most damage was inflicted further north on the mainland, in places like Khao Lak and Krabi, which have been developed more recently. This distinction was not made clear in much of the television coverage, however, with the result that Phuket suffered from a marked lack of visitors for quite a while, even long after most of the damage had been repaired. Advance warning sirens have now been erected on all the main beaches, though fortunately there has been no occasion to sound them.

Though the beaches of Phuket are at their best from mid-November to April, when the sea is calm and rainfall is scant, they are no longer deserted for the remaining months as they once were. Resorts and other attractions now provide plenty to do even when the monsoon winds begin to blow, reaching their peak during August and September.

Right, top: Saltwater swimming pool at Mom Tri's Villa Royale, atop the headland between Kata Yai and Kata Noi beaches. Natural rocks are incorporated into the design.
Right, bottom: Memorial to the victims of the 2004 tsunami, located at Khao Lak on the mainland, which suffered most from the disaster.

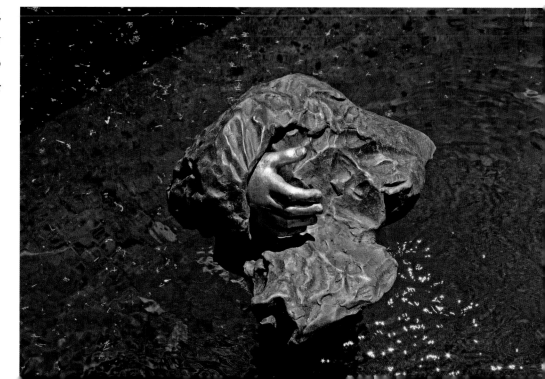

Side Trips Out of Phuket

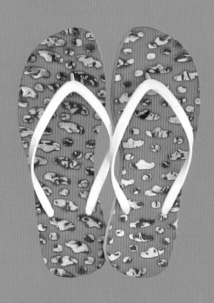

"A number of the islands [in Phang Nga Bay] contain caves, large and small, that can be entered by smaller boats, such as sea canoes, which are increasingly used by advocates of ecotourism."

At the beginning of the 19th century, an American missionary named John Carrington made a trip around what was then known as Monthon Phuket, which included not only the island but a considerable amount of surrounding territory on the mainland. Almost everywhere, he was struck by "the exceeding great beauty" of the landscape and nowhere more so than when he ventured into the magical world of Phang Nga Bay.

Here, he came upon an amazing collection of islands that seemed "to have been pushed right up out of the sea," an experience that inspired a burst of poetic prose. "Such fantastic and charming scenery meets the eye," he later wrote, "wonderful shapes resembling ships, and elephants, and hay stacks, and camels, and dogs, and turrets, and turtles, and kangaroos, and

swans, and bouquets of flowers, at night like specters chasing one another in the sea, the sun setting in the splendor of many colors of blue, and purple, and emerald, and green, and red, and yellow, until the ship carries us away and beyond their sight."

Phang Nga Bay has lost none of its potent appeal and is one of the most popular side trips out of Phuket, some 95 kilometers by road or three hours by boat from the port. The Reverend Carrington was partially right in his geological assumption about the origin of the spectacles. Studies have

Page 37: Dramatic scenery is part of the lure of Phang Nga Bay and nearby Krabi, as this view of Phra Nang Beach suggests. Rock climbing is one of the relatively new sports in the region.
Above: One of Phang Nga Bay's numerous relatively unhabited limestone islands, this one with a secret lake in the center.
Right: Largely deserted beaches on the islands attract tourists, who visit by boat from Phuket or Krabi.

shown that millennia ago, the area was dry land studded with lofty limestone outcrops. As icecaps melted, most recently about 10,000 years ago, sea levels rose and water gradually came in to form the present bay, technically known as "drowned karstland," with only the peaks of the outcrops rising dramatically above the surface. Some are mere rocks, while others tower more than 300 meters, with jungled peaks and sheer cliffsides pockmarked with caves.

He was right, too, about their haunting beauty and evocative configurations, which have inspired a variety of local names for many of the more than 40 islands in the milky green bay. There is, for example, Ko Tapu (Nail Island), which does indeed resemble a slender spike, as well as Ko Khai (Egg Island), Ko Ma Chu (Puppy Island), and Ko Hong (Chamber Island), the latter suggesting a many-roomed apartment building. Khao Phingkan (Leaning Mountain) consists of two separate formations that lean toward one another. It is also commonly referred to as James Bond Island, since it played a role in the popular film *The Man With the Golden Arm* (in which it was supposedly located in China).

A number of the islands contain caves, large and small, that can be entered by smaller boats, such as sea canoes,

Left: Ko Tapu (Nail Island), one of the oddly shaped limestone outcrops that rise in Phang Nga Bay, once dry land before it was flooded by sea-water thousands of years ago.
Right, top: A cave on one of the islands, which can be explored by boats at low tide.
Right, bottom: View of Phang Nga Bay, with its scores of islands rising steeply from milky green waters.

which are being increasingly used by advocates of eco-tourism. At one called Tham Lot, a natural arch festooned with impressive stalactites leads to a cave running for some 50 meters through the entire island, while Tham Kaeo (Glass Cave) is hung with dazzling white stalactites resembling crystal chandeliers. In a cave within Ko Khien (Writing Island) are ancient paintings of sharks, dolphins, and crocodiles, estimated to be between 3,000 and 4,000 years old.

On Ko Pannyi, one of the relatively few inhabited islands, an immense, brooding limestone slab looms over a picturesque Muslim fishing village, complete with a handsome mosque, where some 2,000 people live in a maze of wooden houses on stilts made of tough mangrove wood obtained from the mainland. This has become a major stop for excursion boats, but before tourism provided a significant new source of income, the main industry was the production of pungent shrimp paste, a basic ingredient of Thai cuisine.

The center of the bay is dominated by two large islands, Ko Yao Yai and Ko Yai Noi, both of which have miles of unspoiled beaches and inland areas planted with coconuts, cashews, and rubber trees. Another island of interest is Nakha Noi, home to a company that bills itself as "the only South Sea pearl farm in the world." This is open to the

Left: A daring rock climber gets a bird's-eye view of the Muslim fishing village on Ko Pannyi, one of the few islands in Phang Nga Bay with a permanent population.
Right: Tourist boats explore the picturesque beauties of Phang Nga Bay.

public all year round, and offers tours showing how cultured pearls are produced by placing foreign substances into living oysters and thus triggering the process.

In 1981, Phang Nga Bay was established as a National Park, providing at least some official protection from over-development of tourist facilities and for its wildlife, which includes the pig-tailed macque, a swimming monkey which lives off sea creatures, fruit bats, and some 16 species of birds. Most of the islands are crowned with deciduous lime-stone scrub forest, with taller trees growing in the deeper soil of valleys in some.

Protected from both the northeast and the southwest monsoons, the bay is nearly always calm and can be visit-ed by boat at any season. The best months, though, are from November to May when dependable sunlight ensures the most memorable views of this unforgettable seascape.

Krabi, a province adjacent to Phang Nga, is a more recent destination. Its few but exceptionally fine beaches and natural scenery remained a well-kept secret until only a few years ago, known mainly to backpackers and visiting yachts. This was mainly due to difficulty of access, as there was no local air service and the principal gateway was Phuket, two hours away by road. Now there are direct flights from Bangkok, and Krabi seems poised to experience the questionable pleasures of real estate development.

For the present, though, its broad white-sand beaches, clear waters, and spectacular limestone cliffs remain

A limestone island and visiting boats at Phra Nang Beach in Krabi.

Left: Rayawadee Resort, one of the first facilities in Krabi, consists of pavilions almost hidden in a dense grove of coconut palms.
Opposite, top: Swimming pool at the Rayawadee Resort.
Opposite, bottom: Phra Nang Beach in Krabi, described as one of the most beautiful in the world. It is accessible only by boat.

comparatively unspoiled. The cliffs are popular with intrepid rock climbers, while the beaches draw less athletic escapists determined to share their pleasures with the fewest possible others of their kind. Hat Nang, the longest, on a wide, shallow bay, is easily accessible from the provincial capital and has the most tourist facilities. Some 18 kilometers away is Nopparat Thara Beach, a two-kilometer stretch lined with tall casuarina trees that is part of a national park and likely to be all but empty of visitors.

The most scenic of all in the opinion of some visitors (Britain's *Sunday Times* called it "the second most beautiful beach in the world") is Laem Phra Nang, accessible only by boat. Sheer cliffs and picturesque caves add to the allure of this secret paradise, which is also the site of Krabi's best resort, the Rayawadee, which has won numerous awards for its environmentally friendly design. Some 100 pavilions, furnished with Thai crafts, are scattered through a plantation of towering coconut palms and other indigenous vegetation covering its nine hectares.

Side trips from Laem Phra Nang can be taken to offshore islands as well as to inland destinations like Nam Mao, a 150-meter-high hill with sweeping views; Princess Lagoon, surrounded by tall cliffs and dense vegetation; and a recently discovered cave, Tham Phra Nang Nai, consisting of three chambers filled with unusual limestone formations.

Krabi also includes such locally celebrated sights as Su San Hoi, which has huge slabs composed of fossilized shells estimated at being some 75 million years old; Wat Tham Sua, "Tiger Cave Temple," one of southern Thailand's

most popular monasteries where Buddhist monks meditate in a honeycomb of caves; and Khao Phanom Bencha National Park, 500 square kilometers of primary rain forest with dramatic waterfalls and a great variety of wildlife.

From either Krabi or, more usually, Phuket boats can be hired for a visit to the two Phi Phi islands, part of the 390-square kilometer Ko Phi Phi-Had Nopparat National Park, which rivals Phang Nga Bay as a marine spectacle.

Most of the day trippers head for Phi Phi Don, the larger of the islands, consisting of two irregularly shaped lobes linked by a narrow, sandy isthmus only a few hundred meters wide. Once home to only a small community of Chao Nam this has lost much of its tranquility in recent times, especially at the upper part of Tonsai Bay where the majority of visiting boats land. Restaurants, bungalows, and shops now line the beach here, extending back into the coconut groves beyond. Anyone in search of solitude and quiet is advised to seek it in other areas of the island where there are still superb, almost empty beaches with wonderfully clear waters and excellent opportunities for swimming and snorkeling.

Phi Phi Le is not only less populated but far more spectacular than Phi Phi Don, with its limestone cliffs rising hundreds of meters high out of the sea and its secret coves revealing perfect white-sand beaches with clear waters and

Left: Sheer limestone cliffs have helped turn Krabi into one of the most popular of the newer areas near Phuket.
Right, top: Su San Hoi, where huge slabs are composed of fossilized shells.
Right, bottom: A beach on Tonsai Bay on the Phi Phi Islands, a popular day trip excursion from either Krabi or Phuket.

multitudes of colorful tropical fish. One of these coves, on particularly beautiful Maya Bay, achieved both fame and notoriety a few years ago when it was selected as the chief location for the movie version of *The Beach*, Alex Garland's popular novel about a group of young travelers who create a community in what they perceive as a private Shangri-La, unknown to the outside world. Leonardo Di Caprio and a host of other Hollywood stars and crew members descended on the scenic bay, to the delight of the Tourism Authority but to the dismay of a non-governmental group of environmentalists who launched a noisy campaign against such "improvements" on the natural scenery as planting additional coconut palms and beach shrubbery. The filming went ahead in spite of the protests, and though the result was a resounding flop with critics, it undoubtedly left countless viewers with indelible images of just what the ideal beach ought to look like.

Phi Phi Le is also known for a vast, cathedral-like cavern popularly known as Viking Cave because of its anonymous rock paintings that some think resemble boats used by the ancient Vikings but which are more likely to be Chinese junks painted in the 19th century. The cave is adorned with theatrical stalactites and stalagmites and also contains a shrine where offerings are made by the fearless Chao Nam

Left, top: Scuba diving is one of the most popular diversions in the clear waters around the Phi Phi Islands.
Left, bottom: Two idyllic white-sand beaches are separated by a narrow strip of land on the larger of the Phi Phi Islands.
Right: Clear, turquoise-colored water and limestone cliffs on Phi Phi Don combine to make a memorable impression.

who scale tall, spindly bamboo ladders to collect edible birds' nests deposited on the upper reaches.

These nests, which are found on several islands in the area, have long been a source of great profit to the companies granted a license by the government to collect them. They are produced by a tiny, fork-tailed swift called *Callocalia esculenta* which, as if aware of their value, builds them at great heights and in the least accessible places. Cup-shaped and small, only about 3–4 centimeters in diameter, the nests are constructed from a gluey secretion discharged by two glands under the bird's lower jaw. This emerges in long strands that harden into a strong substance on exposure to the air.

Just how and when the Chinese acquired an insatiable taste for the nests is unknown, but it was certainly centuries ago. One legend says they were discovered by a group of shipwrecked sailors on an island, while another asserts that a eunuch sent by one of the Ming emperors to the Malay Peninsula was so impressed by their medicinal powers that he brought some back to his homeland. In any event, the use of the nests in a savory soup became a major Chinese culinary achievement, one often baffling to Western gourmets but still as highly regarded as ever in China itself, where they are believed to be nourishing, to cure a number of ailments ranging from upset stomachs to measles, and, most important of all, to delay senility and promote virility.

Left: Phra Nang Beach, with dense jungle coming down almost to the sandy shore.
Right: Birds' nest collector walking across a precarious bamboo bridge to enter the Viking Cave on Phi Phi Le, where ancient rock paintings adorn the walls and coveted birds' nests are harvested from the upper reaches.

Nests are divided into three categories according to quality and time of collection. The highest, usually obtained only in the first harvest, are the purest and contain the least amount of foreign material. Somewhat lower down on the scale are "red nests," so-called because they have a reddish tinge caused by twigs eaten by the bird. At the bottom of the scale are "black nests," which contain a good deal of foreign matter that must be removed before they are eaten. These are further subdivided into some ten categories and priced accordingly.

In Thailand, concessions to collect the nests are granted to only a few companies, who then process, package, and market them. Harvesting takes place seasonally, allowing the birds time to reproduce. In places like the cave on Phi Phi Le, it is done by men who pass on the skill from generation to generation. It is a hazardous task requiring steely nerves and an ability to often work in total darkness or by the light of a flickering candle attached to a cap. The effort, though, is well worth it for both the collecting companies and the millions of Chinese all of the world eagerly awaiting this rare delicacy.

Another destination, about 100 kilometers northwest of Phuket in the Andaman Sea, is Ko Similan National Park, which has been described as 'Thailand's most beautiful and unspoiled marine national park." (The name Similan derives from the Malay word *sembilan*, meaning "nine," the number of islands that comprise the group.) It takes more than 10 hours by motor boat to reach the Similans from Phuket, so several days must be allowed for an excursion, often using the boat

itself as a floating hotel during the visit or staying in one of the few simple bungalows provided by the Royal Forestry Department on Ko Miang. For serious scuba divers and snorkelers, however, the long trip is worth the effort and expense, since the Similans are celebrated for the more than 200 species of coral, colorful tropical fish, and other varieties of marine life to be found in their turquoise waters.

This was more true 30-odd years ago than it is today. Then, almost the only visitors were a few Chao Nam, or

Opposite: Rocky coastlines with coves of clear water characterize the Similan Islands, now part of a protected national park northwest of Phuket. **Above:** One of the countless unspoiled beaches that await visitors to the Similan Islands.

This page: The clear waters around the Similan Islands harbor masses of brightly colored tropical fish as well as delicate coral formations, making them a prized destination for scuba divers. Declaring the islands a marine national park and banning commercial fishing boats has helped reduce damage to the reefs.

Opposite: Intricate sea fans add to the underwater spectacle awaiting divers in the Similans.

so-called Sea Gypsies, who came to fish the teeming reefs, and a very occasional yacht bringing adventurous outsiders. The almost total isolation changed with Phuket's rapid development as a tourist center and as more and more commercial fishing trawlers began coming to the islands. Alarmed by the destructive effects that followed, particularly the dynamiting of reefs by fishermen, the government declared the Similans a marine national park in 1982, banned trawlers, and took other steps to protect the environment. While this has not entirely stopped the problem, it has certainly reduced it and helped preserve the reefs for the pleasure of future generations.

Divers will discover an extraordinary underwater world of submerged peaks, canyons, and swim-through tunnels encrusted with hard and soft coral, fish of all kinds, and such marine life as huge sea fans, sea urchins, and barrel sponges. The best surviving reefs are on the western side of the islands, where they slope gradually into deeper sea and are thus less susceptible to damage by large fishing boats. Onshore, while the scenery is less spectacular than that to be seen in the Phi Phi Islands, there is a rich variety of wildlife. Sea turtles come to lay their eggs on the sandy beach of Ko Hu Yong, the longest beach in the park, though their numbers have been declining in recent years. There are also crab-eating monkeys, dusky langurs, and around 30 confirmed bird species, including the white-bellied sea eagle and the Nicobar pigeon.

The best time for visiting the Similans is from December to April, when the sea is generally calm and clear.

Phuket's Inland Attractions

"The most visible reflection of the faith followed by nearly all Thais, the *wat* or monastery, is a striking architectural creation, with multilayered tiered roofs and a profusion of ornate decoration that often reaches heights of dazzling fantasy."

While the great majority of visitors to Phuket are likely to spend their time on one of its alluring beaches, with perhaps a shopping trip into the provincial capital on a rainy day, there are a number of other attractions for those who want a somewhat broader view of the island. Here are a few worth seeking out:

Khao Phra Taew Royal Wildlife Forest Reserve. Located in the northern part of the island, down a road leading from Thalang, this is the last sizeable part of the dense evergreen rain forest that once covered most of Phuket. It is centered around three mountains of various heights and contains lofty trees, some up to 40 meters tall and supported by dramatic buttress roots, forming a canopy that filters sunlight down to a luxuriant selection of humidity-loving palms, ferns, and lower plants. Of particular note is *Karedoxa dolphin*, popularly known as the white-backed palm, a fan-shaped variety on which the underside of the leaf is silver

colored. This is a rare species found only on Phuket Island and a few places on the mainland.

Trails lead through the forest, and the lucky hiker may catch a glimpse of the shy gibbons, slow loris, mouse deer, and other wildlife that have sought refuge there. A popular attraction in the forest reserve with locals, particularly on weekends, is Tone Sai Waterfall, which, it must be admitted, really lives up to its name only during the rainy season.

Buddhist Temples. The most visible reflection of the faith followed by nearly all Thais, the *wat* or monastery, is a striking architectural creation, with multilayered tiled roofs and a profusion of ornate decoration that often reaches heights of dazzling fantasy. None of Phuket's 30-odd temples can approach the splendor of those to be seen in Bangkok or Chiang Mai, but nevertheless several are worth a visit by anyone interested in the local culture.

Wat Chalong, on the road leading from the town to several of the west coast beaches, is the largest and best known. Especially on Buddhist holidays, large numbers of people come to make offerings of floral garlands and incense sticks to the principal image. One of the buildings also enshrines statues of two celebrated 19th-century monks named Luang Pho Chaem and Luang Pho Chuang, who

Page 58: Parasailing, one of the many water sports available on popular Patong Beach.
Page 59: The glittering, multitiered roofs of Wat Chalong, Phuket's largest Buddhist temple.
Left: A multistoried structure at Wat Chalong, which covers a large area and displays many of the distinctive architectural features of Thai Buddhist temples.
Right: Devotees pay respect to images of revered monks at Wat Chalong. Offerings or floral garlands and incense sticks are made on such occasions.

helped put down a rebellion by Chinese miners in 1876 and who are still honored by today's residents.

Another important temple is Wat Phra Thong, a few kilometers north of Thalang on the airport road. This is built around a gilded (popular belief says solid gold) Buddha image half buried in the ground. According to legend, this was discovered by a farmer whose efforts to uncover the remainder of the image proved fruitless. Instead, he built a shelter over the torso and this eventually became the temple, which has been frequently enlarged and refurbished over the years.

Wat Phra Nang Sang, in Thalang, is one of Phuket's oldest. It was there in 1785 when the Burmese invaded and some of the fighting supposedly took place in the temple grounds. The Burmese were allegedly looking for a manuscript that would guide them to buried treasure but failed to find it. Enshrined at the temple are three enormous images made of tin, the precious metal that provided most of the island's early wealth. In Phuket Town, the most prominent temple is Wat Mongkol Nim, a large monastery built in Rattanakosin (or Bangkok) style, which displays some finely carved doors.

Mosques. Though mostly small, these are common on Phuket, especially in seaside areas. The largest is near predominantly Muslim Surin Beach, an impressive structure

Left: Wat Phra Nang Sang, an ornately decorated temple at Thalang, is one of the oldest and most often restored of Phuket's monasteries.
Right: The principal Buddha image at Wat Phra Nang Sang, displayed on a high altar with a mural painting of a bodhi tree on the wall behind.

Above: Entrance to the main theater at FantaSea, modeled after the famous temple of Angkor Wat, where a lavish show is staged featuring elephants and spectacular effects.
Left: A beautiful Thai girl in a traditional costume entices visitors to enjoy a ride in a trishaw around FantaSea.

with four minarets around a central domed building. It is crowded with the faithful every Friday, the Muslim holy day.

Phuket Museum. Although it was opened in 1987, near the Heroines Monument on the airport road, this has never managed to accumulate a collection of any great interest. Most of the exhibits consist of old weapons, photographs, and a few historical artifacts found in the Thalang area.

Shell Museum. This is a private enterprise located just north of Rawai on the road leading to Phuket Town. It displays an interesting collection of seashells, including what is purported to be the world's largest golden pearl and an enormous shell weighing 250 kilograms. Most of the shells were found in the waters off the island, though some come from elsewhere in Thailand. The exhibits are attractively arranged and labeled in both English and Thai.

FantaSea. Imagine Las Vegas at its most extravagant, with a touch of Disneyland and a dose of Thai culture thrown in for good measure, and you have some idea of what to expect at this popular attraction near Kamala Beach.

The main theater, seating some 3,000 people, vaguely resembles a temple at Angkor, surrounded by souvenir shops, game parlors of various kinds, and a gigantic restaurant that serves surprisingly good Thai, Chinese, Japanese and Western food. The show has just about everything—realistic onstage battles, acrobats descending from the ceiling, magic acts,

Pool of golden carp in the FantaSea complex, adorned with figures from Thai mythology.

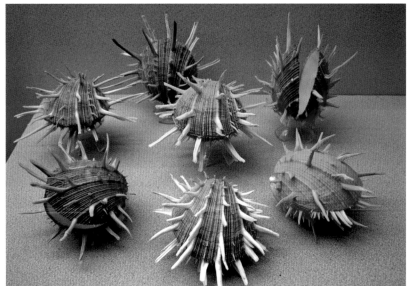

Clockwise from top left: Entrance to the Gibbon Rehabilitation Center, where young captive gibbons are reintroduced to life in the wide; Shell Museum, where local shells are displayed; spiny jewel-like shells on display; gibbons in cages awaiting their freedom.

comedy, classical Thai legend and, most memorable of all, some 30 elephants, whose silent entry down the aisles is truly thrilling. It sounds over the top, and it is, but so professionally lit and executed that it is guaranteed to appeal to all ages.

Phuket Butterfly Garden and Aquarium. Children will enjoy this and possibly parents as well. Located about three kilometers outside of town, on Highway 402, it has thousands of multicolored butterflies in a huge net enclosure and aquariums displaying live coral and various kinds of tropical fish.

Gibbon Rehabilitation Center. Turn left at the Heroines Monument on the way in from the airport, go around nine kilometers toward the east coast, and follow a signposted road to Bang Pae Falls. Here, at a facility founded by wildlife conservationists, young gibbons who have been rescued from captivity are reintroduced to life in their native forest.

Chinese Temples. Not surprisingly, in view of its history, Phuket has numerous Chinese shrines and temples, gaudily decorated in red and gold, fragrant with the smoke of countless burning incense sticks, and often displaying huge images of various gods and goddesses. The principal one is at Kathu, where the Vegetarian Festival originated, while in town the largest are Bang Niew, devoted to the deities Siew, Hok, and Lok, who represent longevity, power, and happiness, and Jui Tui, dedicated to the vegetarian god Ku Wong and noted as a place to have fortunes read.

Right, top: Entrance to the Phuket Aquarium, located close to the port near the provincial capital.
Right, bottom: Phuket Zoo, where monkeys and other animals are popular with younger visitors.

National Festivals. Phuket's only purely local celebration is the Chinese Vegetarian Festival, described elsewhere in this book, but all of the national ones are observed as well. The biggest are Songkran, the traditional Thai New Year, which is held in mid-April and involves both religious ceremonies and much high-spirited water throwing, and Loy Krathong, on the full-moon night of the 11th lunar month (usually October or early November) when little boats in the shape of lotus flowers are set adrift, each carrying a lighted candle, incense sticks, and flowers.

There are also several major Buddhist celebrations, designated as national holidays, when temples are particularly crowded. Like Loy Krathong, these are lunar events and the timing varies from year to year. The most important is Visaka Puja, commemorating the Buddha's birth, enlightenment, and death, which generally falls in May. Makha Puja, in February, recalls the miraculous assembly of 1,250 disciples who assembled without warning to pay the Buddha homage. Asala Puja, in July, marks the Buddha's first sermon, followed the next day by Khao Pansa, the start of the three-month Rains Retreat when monks must stay in their monasteries to study and practice meditation. Most of these include solemn, candle-lit processions around the main building of the temple after dark.

Left, top: Chinese lighting candles at a temple during the annual Vegetarian Festival, held in October.
Left, bottom: Fireworks create a haze as well as a din during the Vegetarian Festival parade.

Above: Spectacular displays of self-mutilation have become a feature of the Vegetarian Festival.

Right: Participants in the festival traditionally wear white outfits. One of Phuket's many Chinese temples can be seen in the background.

"Southern food in general is as distinctive as the region's scenery. In addition to the herbs and spices used in most parts of the country ... it also contains seasonings that reflect foreign influences.... Water sports of just about every kind are available on most Phuket beaches, from swimming to others calling for more specialized skills."

Visiting Phuket

The island of Phuket is a dream destination for visitors worldwide, whether they want an action-packed holiday or a relaxing break. Apart from the island's incomparable sun-drenched beaches and out-of-this-world resorts, Phuket's many events and festivals, its daring-do water sports and superb golf courses, and its lively nightlife and entertainment can make the difference between a good and a really memorable holiday. Not forgetting the food and the shopping!

Thai food is now enjoying a vogue almost everywhere in the world, from London and Sydney to New York and Paris, and probably most visitors arrive with at least some experience of its best-known creations like Pad Thai (stir-fried noodles with shrimp or chicken) or Tom Yam Goong (hot and sour shrimp soup), both of which occur in numerous versions. What many may not

realize is that Thai food varies from region to region and the dish they enjoyed at the restaurant back home is likely to be quite different when they order it in Phuket.

Southern food in general is as distinctive as the region's scenery. In addition to the herbs and spices used in most parts of the country—chili peppers, ginger, garlic, lemongrass, kaffir lime, coriander, and the like—it also contains seasonings that reflect foreign influences. Gaeng Massaman, for example, is more reminiscent of an Indian curry than a Thai one, involving cardamom, cloves, and cinnamon and either chicken or beef (but never pork), while there are several Malayan fish curries, often with a garnish of fresh fruit, and Satay, marinated pieces of beef or chicken on skewers served with a spicy peanut sauce, which originally came from Indonesia. In view of Phuket's history, it should come as no surprise that Chinese influences are strong, though often given a distinctive Thai flavor.

Also not surprisingly, the ubiquitous coconut plays a prominent role in many dishes. Its milk tempers the heat of chili-laced soups and curries (which tend to be hotter

Page 71: Pristine Railay Beach, one of the many attractions of Krabi, with a background of limestone cliffs. With improved transportation, Krabi has become one of the more popular destinations near Phuket.
Left: A bowl of spicy seafood soup, a southern delicacy. The ornately decorated bowl is a ware known as *bencharong* ("five colors"), which was originally made in China for export to Thailand but is now widely produced locally for more upmarket restaurants.
Right: A selection of southern dishes and ingredients, among them grilled meat on skewers, southern-style curries, shredded papaya salad, and assorted chili peppers. Southern food varies in flavor from that in other parts of Thailand and borrows elements from other Asian cultures, such as Malaysia, Indonesia, and India.

in the south than in any other region, with the possible exception of the northeast), its oil is often used for frying, and its grated flesh serves as a condiment. Also only to be expected is the abundance of fresh seafood from the surrounding waters: marine fish, some of huge size, shrimps, crabs, squid, scallops, clams, mussels, and rock lobsters. The last has become popular only in relatively recent years, in part due to the demand for it by foreign visitors.

Southerners are partial to a bitter flavor in their cooking, particularly when it is supplied by a flat bean called sa-taw, not always so esteemed by outsiders, whether foreign or Thai. Europeans, at least, often take a similar view of the southern durian which, like those of Malaysia, tends to be much more assertive in taste and smell than the comparatively mild varieties found in Bangkok markets.

But if the celebrated prickly, football-sized fruit—described by one Westerner as "the prince of fruits to those who like it but the chief of abominations to all strangers and novices"—fails to appeal, there are plenty of others on Phuket menus to compensate. Among these are pineapples of exceptional sweetness, mangoes, papayas, mangosteens, rambutans, rose apples, and delectable little "finger bananas" which, either deep-fried or boiled in coconut milk, make a delicious dessert.

Left: Textiles and other handicrafts from various parts of Thailand, especially the northeast and the far north, can be found on sale in Phuket, as in this shop at Mom Tri's Boathouse.
Right, top and bottom: A colorful array of items are available at sidewalk stalls in Phuket Town, mostly brought in by enterprising dealers from other regions.

In addition to Thai food, Phuket has numerous excellent Chinese restaurants, especially in the town, as well as others representing just about every other national cuisine, including French and Italian.

Aside from items fashioned from seashells, some of considerable beauty, Phuket is not noted for its local handicrafts. This does not means the island is a shopping Sahara, however, for enterprising merchants have filled their shelves with products from all over the country, especially those from Chiang Mai in the far north. Fine textiles such as lustrous silk and supple cotton are abundantly available, as well as wood carvings, silverware, jewelry, gemstones. lacquer, and antiques of dubious provenance but undeniable beauty. The widest selection is probably to be found in Phuket Town or at Patong, but almost every beach has shops of some kind to tempt buyers.

Water sports of just about every kind are available on most Phuket beaches, from swimming to others calling for more specialized skills. Scuba diving is one of the most popular, thanks to the rich variety of underwater life, and there are numerous qualified instructors to teach newcomers how to master the techniques of this rewarding activity with the proper equipment. Sailboats, catamarans, and full-sized live-aboard yachts can also be hired by the day or

Left: Water sports of all kinds are popular in Phuket, among them parasurfing, like this daring exhibition on Patong Beach.
Right: Yachts from all over the world assemble at Phuket during the annual King's Cup Regatta, held at the beginning of December. Victorious crews are fond of celebrating with a champagne toast, like this festive group at Kata Beach.

chartered for longer trips to outlying islands. For the less energetic, Chinese junks and other luxurious craft, complete with crew, are available for sunset cruises around the island. In addition, several companies based in Phuket offer trips by inflatable kayaks that can enter semisubmerged caves inaccessible to larger boats. Other popular sports include deep-sea fishing, parasailing, waterskiing, banana boating, and, during certain seasons when the waves are high, excellent surfing.

Several superb Phuket golf courses have attracted noted players like Tiger Woods for championship playoffs. More hardy adventurers may prefer rock climbing, especially in Krabi where more than 450 separate climbs have been identified and chartered, and daredevils can test their nerve on one of the bungee jumps enterprising operators have set up in recent years (so far, it is comforting to report, with a 100 percent safety rate).

The two biggest organized sporting events on the island are the King's Cup Regatta, held over several days to mark the King's birthday in early December, and the Phuket Triathlon, held in the Laguna Phuket area in October, which features 1.8 kilometers of swimming, 55 kilometers of cycling, and 12 kilometers of jogging.

Left: One of Phuket's numerous world-class golf courses, many of them built on formerly barren stretches that were once open tin mines.
Right, top and bottom: The King's Cup Regatta, honoring His Majesty's birthday on December 5, has become a major annual event, attracting a colorful fleet of international contestants whose elegant sails can be seen over several days. A representative of the King presents the winning trophy on the final evening of the competition.